Unlocatable Source

Unlocatable Source

Poems by Judith Bowles

Turning Point

For dear Chet. —
When friendship
is a treasure we want
to have, always.
With love,
Judy

Published by Turning Point
P.O. Box 541106
Cincinnati, OH 45254-1106

ISBN: 978-1-62549-316-3

Poetry Editor: Kevin Walzer
Business Editor: Lori Jareo

Visit us on the web at www.turningpointbooks.com

Acknowledgments

Better Than Starbucks: "Keyhole"

Bloedel Reserve: "Forsythia"

Cobalt Review: "Untitled Poem"

Ekphrastic Review: "The Pianist and the Poet"

"On First Reading Li Young Li's *Eating Together*"

"The Flying Carriage"

Gargoyle: "Non-Catholic Girl"

Innisfree Journal of Poetry: "Left Behind"

To my Grandchildren:
Henry, Charlie, Eli, Grace, and Fia

Table of Contents

Introduction

The painter Edward Hopper was interested in the unnoticed though extraordinary qualities of existence; his desire was, as he once said, just to paint sunlight draped along the side of a house. He also said that there would be no need for visual art if we could adequately put all of this into words. The obverse side of that coin is true, too. There would be no need for poetry if we could paint our way back toward the unlocatable source of our character and its obsessions with such light and shadow.

I have long felt the poetry of Judith Bowles was the counterpart to Hopper. In her new collection, we find the same lone figures staring out of windows and gazing from front porches, narrated by a poet whose influences could be traced in a lineage from Merwin and Strand, to Stevens and the Symbolists of the 19th century.

Judith Bowles is a poet of huge gifts, and this book, her finest, is the marvelous culmination of a life of looking and listening with intent self-awareness, and with unquenchable love for the world. "It went very dark in the back of the car," she writes in the masterful "Left Behind." It is the outer realms of the work, Hopper used to say, that always reflect the inner realms of the worker. Inasmuch as Bowles' poetry describes the world in its mysteries and silences, she is mapping a darker region of the self all the time. What does the voice sound like, when it is here to give shape to the silence in the house, interrupted only now and then by tragedy or outcry? When the poet has gone very deep and very far, it sounds like this.

David Keplinger
Washington, DC 2019

One

…I glimpsed an elsewhere of potential which seemed at the same time to be a somewhere being remembered.

—Seamus Heaney

Untitled Poem

Not finding the grave of my parents
I came down the road of misshapen trees whose
roots, strangled, shoved up in a mass and a heave.
Earth there is parched and speaks, with an effort, of days
filled with birds, of the many shades of memorial green.
I am getting rid of some clothes that clutter my mind
with their endless stripes and misshapen sleeves.
Two bags full hope that this riddance makes room
for some grammar to settle, finally, and offer the handhold,
the intricate balance that aerial footing requires.
Not finding my untitled poem this morning was like the mass
and the heave of the earth, parched but still speaking,
and it told me so.

Correspondences

An allée of soft pines my father planted
on one of the multiple hills in southern Ohio,
to frame his shooting range, hid him
behind the cabin he called Possum Run.
A place, he said, would add years to his life.

The trees gathered sparrows busy
being together, their flitting a song in itself.
They rose in an urgent communion,
a breath taken up and released,
when the shot cracked the air.

It was sound being seen, this rush and rise,
an explosion in air of a hundred hearts
beating together and moving together
like a story being told by a chorus
about one lonely man.

Next Poem

It hovers
    a perpetual buzz
from an unlocatable source
    like eternity

and floats just above struggle
    itself while the weight of work wisdom
the pain of specific gravity
    gather force in *this* poem…

full of confusion
    about even the flowers
that cluster the pear tree
    with their grandmother-laden fragrance…

and why the pills
    in a row on the counter
are a rag-tag army
    ready to fight…

and the tulips askew
    in the big-bottomed vase

hold their sunsetty bloom
    as if…

The next poem will know
    will clutch and catch
what is just out of reach
    with implacable force

Pictures with Stories

Who cared what pictures my Grandmother Bessie
pasted with mixed flour and water and smoothed
on each page of the tasseled green scrapbook
but Aunt Myrna and me? And now only me
by default since I learned that Riggs girls
don't last forever, nor the things they hold dear.

The Dionne quintuplets are gathered here,
a litter of girls that gave comfort. Bessie's five
came single file and were prettier by far
than those spooky-eyed babies the world
gawked at through glass in their cribs.
Together they smile at their first year's candle.

When Princess Elizabeth with brown curly hair
became Queen of all England her crown
found a home beyond Westminster walls.
Even Brookville, PA, felt its weight. The Queen
is shown changing a tire and walking through mud
like regular people are meant to do.

Her book carried pictures with stories
that said other women's lives, no matter their
famous good fortune, were full of the struggles
she knew. Jeannette MacDonald sang
seven days a week for the troops
but never married the love of her life.

Bessie got strict when needed and instead
of calling her five by name: Myrna, Grace, Dorothy,
Frances, Jo— *girlie girl* sliced through the air.
When she was dying and thought she'd been robbed,
Grace told her no, only her daughters were there.
Listen up, girlie girl, I know what I know.

My Father Explains

A blind man came for dinner
to our house. My father described
the plate that sat before him
as if it were a clock.

Chicken would be at 3, potatoes
at 6, peas at 9. The man shut his eyes
and smiled at a lesson so clearly stated
that you would almost have to

be blind to imagine.
I wondered when the man
shut his eyes was he picturing
my father blind

to give himself company
in the world where he lived.
I shut my eyes and so did my brother
and we tried to eat without seeing.

Echo Chamber

Wood paneled my father's study,
a sturdy oak table with heavy turned legs,
books like unclimbable mountains squeezed on shelves,
or wide open on its own slanted table, all

three-thousand, three-hundred and fifty
papery thin pages of Webster's International.
Leaded glass windows erased trees to shadowy
shapes; faded to blonde, the head and arms of the brown

leather chair. And on a small table to the side of the chair,
his Dictaphone, cone on a cord in my hand, I sat cushioned
and ready to nearly sing with Annabelle Lee. She was a child
and I was a child. These were words I was ready to own

at the press of a little red button. It seemed purely me
over and over, sound swelling and cadenced beyond
my own ken, my senses leaping in a newfound expanse.
A tiny needle like a doll's sewing machine

etched grooves into the cylinder where my voice
skidded and settled, and another button,

black, brought it up out of the cone like an echo chamber.
From this dazzle of possibility

came small, watery unstirred words,
heavy urgent breaths, and perhaps most woeful of all,
a monotonous sing-song version that lost me
to Anabelle Lee.

My Father Mowing the Lawn

My house was on a hill.
The front yard sloped down to the road.
The back yard was flat.

As a child I thought things
had always been as they were.
Would always be as they were.

Even the trees.
The catalpa by the driveway in the front yard.
Its giant memorial leaves.

The privet hedge at the side of the house.
It was a monument too
That outlined forever the turn up the hill.

The basement, the coal bin, the rec room,
the shuffle board court out back.
All impervious to change.

My father's habits rose like the sun every day,
he set out for the hospital, dressed and shined

and became who I was told he was.

The catalpa grew and its huge flowers turned
into leathery pods. My father never came home to us
the way I saw men in movies coming home from work

their jackets hooked over their shoulder,
their collars loosened, open, ready to laugh.
I wondered if it made a man unimportant

to like his family. Occasionally
my father mowed the front lawn. The push mower
rhythm was set by the turn of the wheels,

a hesitant moment then a quick whirring rush
except when it jammed from a stick.
Something was on display when this impeccable

man mowed the lawn shirtless, his mat of chest hair
lay against his skin like barbed wire,
his underwear hung out from his shorts.

The lawn was well kept. He never looked up.
We never quite learned how to talk to each other.
All of us lonely we weren't sure for whom.

Atlantis—A Question

I left jam on the page while I read in the A's
how Atlantis sank in the sea

then tried with a wet cloth to wipe it off. The paper
dissolved and tore

in my frantic attempt to set time backwards
before my unknowing finger

had brushed the place where Atlantis followed
Atlantic Standard Time.

Now I'll always remember the name
of the island that sank

the way that my kneecaps surrounded by bathwater
sat like two crowns

before they got slowly drowned while I watched
and wrote words

in the tiny bubbles lining my legs. The way water
inched up was a lesson I loved

to learn every time. And what was Atlantis to me
anyway, where everything went under

and never came up? Like a funeral where they say
gone but not forgotten.

What good was remembering
if they always stayed dead?

Close to My Side

After mistaking a biker, head down, for a horse
on the path coming toward me
I wondered how to greet it; to stop, step aside
or hold my own place and reach for her muzzle
as I would have done with my pinto pony,
my cheek on her neck.

The hunched-over biker whizzed by and I kept to my path.
My pony was white, scattered with brown as if someone
had emptied a bucket of paint over her in the wind.
She nodded her head when I came in the stall
and kept close to my side, nudging me with her nose
as if to say *Listen. I'm ready to go.*

In the cold, before we headed out for the trail
I warmed her up bareback around the ring.
I tried every day to get enough, put my face in her mane
for the ocean of her, that strong neck a wave rising
ready to arrive.

The Broken Bike

It's hard to tell about Joe's bike
because it was broken before it broke down.
This is really a story about a brother and sister
who could never fix anything. And they knew it.

The bike was black and Joe had to twist the handlebars
to the left to make the tires go straight. The crooked seat
was a dangerous perch, half of one pedal was gone.
Mornings he tore down our driveway on its rickety wheels

with nobody watching
and only our catalpa tree's
giant leaves showed his breeze.

What happened is it fell apart one day
with me on the fender behind my brother
going up the hill. I jumped off when the front wheel
wobbled and the whole thing collapsed under his legs.

The parts took on a new frenzied life like a giant
magnet was rearranging them on the road
and then they were still and we stood over them

not even astonished at the ruins around us.

No one else at our school had a capital letter inside
their name. I said we were French a long time ago
and then we left home. It felt like the truth.
I carried the wheels, Joe took the rest.

Left Behind

We had grown used to the sand
and hot stones
under our feet, the salty taste of our towels, the strange
little houses we all stayed in that faced each other
with slamming screen doors and wide open windows.
And how everything there in Florida
happened outside.
When my brother and I
grew used to that house—
Where our mother had brought us to get healthy again—
foam on the ocean was a cloud dipping down
that tickled our feet and made a soft sink.
I carried that thought back from the beach
and slept with it.
My fourth birthday
brought large, flat paper presents that got left behind
In the wide open house. Something bad happened
to my aunt and we had to go home one night.
It went very dark in the back of the car.

From the Deep to the Shallow

When we watched older kids climb
the high-diving board, suspend into space
and then splash, we screamed, grabbed
a friend, ducked her under.

My wild leap onto Lois sent her under
and up in a bloody-nosed fury.
The guard's long urgent whistle
I thought was for me, but a second

one signaled to get out of the pool.
They dragged a body from the deep
to the shallow. His name
was Dick Knight. Dick Knight.

The edge of the pool had a green shiny lip
slippery under our feet.
It was home base for the wet-hearted games
nobody but us ever played.

Keyhole

when your name is announced coffee comes

in a paper cup beside a box crammed

with collars to buffer your fingers

from the heat which finds its way through

and the palm nestles into its ease while you check

the black lid is clipped all around

and the keyhole at the edge looks up and is ready

for the first tiny sip when the tongue makes its test

the way my hand pulled my mother's coat

over my face and knew its button hole

that opened and shut was the safe way to dose

the world to myself

Stay For a While

Stay for a while on one solid image
filled with the colors of marigolds
in tiny trays waiting beside my kneeling mother
who rocks back and forth as she digs into earth
her trowel conducting a softening sound
that repeats in a very small circle. Then the gentle
lifting of each tiny plant, with the hands of a nurse
who knows how to move without causing harm.

Cold takes hold of Ohio earth and turns it
to stone in the winter
changes the shape of our front yard catalpa
where icicles hang like seedpods
and the northern side of the tree has frozen
its dusting of snow.
My mother is coming up the iced, glassy steps to the door
her frosted breath heavy as if it were laden
with smoke or something more dense,
her two sisters' suicides.

There will be no thaw
come the spring when green presses forth

toward the light as it should.

The cold's settled into the bones of our house.

The catalpa sends its mass of white open-

mouthed flowers into bloom, one piling on top

of the other, too many to count and then foot-

long pods, soft green and fringed, hang on

while the seeds ripen into wings.

In the Dark

We made ourselves small. Even our breath.
We knew to be safe.
We laughed in the night, emptied our *light*
all over the cave where it sunk in the walls
that were moist with our life. We became stones.
We knew how they spoke, their colors
so subtle, so different, the one from the other
that only a stone could read what was there.
We spelled out our names on the wall.
My brother is scattered in units
of blaze, beyond the language of caves
and the fortress we built in the dark.

The Flying Carriage

Marc Chagall, 1913

When he couldn't see Vitebsk from his doorstep
Chagall climbed a little post. When he needed more
he did what his grandfather did to eat his carrots. He climbed
up on the roof. Home was a place to be owned
by wide watching.

There is a fire at the heart of the scene in his painting
coming from a tiny house
that spills its color like a highway
for the eye to follow. A man walks it toward the doorstep.
He rocks a white pail of water and maybe hears his wife

calling from the dark edge toward a palette of stones
that might carry her across to him. They are staying
in the flaming frame but the carriage with the black horse
lifting is leaving. The driver, dazzled to his task,
flings his arms into an arc.

A ladder leans against the roof of the house
which makes a place for sitting and watching
an ecstasy in motion away from danger.

Lake

All by ourselves
in the lake water dark
we came close to drowning.
Nothing held me up.
My feet lost their place.
Water took my breath.
Lake of my heart,
Uncle Jack's wet Sunday suit
made me sick from its closet smell.
His arms were hard
and held us too tight
my brother and I said later
showing each other
our bruises.

I Wrote My Brother

I wrote my brother Joe's thank-you letters.
Someone had to do it.
Mother meant someone other than him
always which was me.
I couldn't imagine not doing something
that needed to be done
so I wrote them and here's how it worked:

I counted 5 red lines on the stationery pad
to fill and no more which was a rule.
I made up a brother in my mind
who might say he really liked the gift
of a walkie-talkie. Then by line 3
he said how he and I sent messages
from room to room. I wanted to say more

that we made up characters to be
how his was Joe Palooka, mine Judy Canova
but that was line 5 and I'd used
up the space.
Always felt my heart

do a strange little dance after that

for the fun of the gift we'd been given.

Magic

Tongue knows burrowing and teaches the hands
to explore what they need not see
like this child knows how to find what's in the dirt.
Her friend says they both know what hidden magic
would rise up when they let it know they are there.
They dig bending close to the earth, to each other.

The girl is little but she knows there is no other
part of her body that can dance like her hands.
She tells her arms to let them be there
and they flounce in the air to see
if a song might arise that would match the magic
she hears every night dreaming of dirt.

She wonders about her father in a box under the dirt.
The girl hears a sound every night like other
voices telling her secrets and then like magic
they turn into earthworms that squirm in her hands.
She wonders as they writhe can they see?
Do they know she and her hands are there?

Her friend is burying his goldfish there
deep through stones to another layer of dirt.
It had lived by his bed for years and could see
daylight before he woke up. It was like no other
fish and its fins waved him into the day like hands.
His father put him by the bed and called him Magic.

He told the boy to keep his eyes open for magic
because, like the fish, it was always there
but also, not something you could hold in your hands.
Maybe it should still be in water not dirt.
This friend tells him: dead life should go in the dirt.
He cries that its eyes can no longer see.

The children are doing something they don't want to see.
This search is a dark one. They both know that magic
needs help. One digs to find a father, the other
to find a place his fish will be safe. They are there
bringing now to the place that moments ago was just dirt.
The hole is wide and deep, smoothed by their hands.

The fish, quiet in a matchbox, is laid down with soft hands
and the friend says how he wants it held always there
sort of snug. It might learn to breathe; it is Magic.

Every Tuesday

The static of traffic reminds me that life goes on
no matter how it stops in its tracks when your father dies
and suddenly dead is inside your door taking breath
out of every step while the dew rises along with the sun
and someone is dragging their trash can to the curb
for a truck to wheeze into place and receive
and the driver is waving to the small boy who runs to the door
every Tuesday for the thrill of the racket in front of his house
then chases his dog, Tillie, who escaped into the yard
and races after a squirrel who scurries up a tree
and mid climb looks at the dog, twitching and scornful.

Two

"Says I to myself" should be the motto of my journal. It is fatal to the writer to be too much possessed by his thought. Things must lie a little remote to be described.

—Henry David Thoreau, The Journal, 1837-1861

Come Back Tomorrow *

She wonders while holding the towel against her heart
how the melody keeps hold of the sweet violin
how Scheherazade keeps hold of her song suspended in time
on a slender thread. The laundry is heavy and damp
deep in the machine and clings like reluctant children
who want to stay but the storied music reaches down
to her hands for the lifting
shaking and heaving into the dryer wide open
the hollow sound of the door, the percussive thump
of rotating wetness. She thinks of the Princess
who weaves surprise and suspense with the sensual
ease of a snake charmer under threat of the morning
and a knock at the door. The music comes close to a goal
then veers to go elsewhere that is somehow connected.
The dryer felt warm and the load would grow lighter.

*Words of the Sultan to the executioner who appears every morning to execute his wife,
Scheherazade.

Incidental Music

My mother sang sad songs to us
and when I wept, as I always did
she said *it was only a song.*
But I had heard the hollow mourning.

Her Pennsylvania roots were tangled
by the rocks they had to grow against
in the underground weather of the earth.
Twisted trees show their story.

I laugh when I hear birds at the edge of our woods.
My mother would have too.
She knew the urgency of a pulse
beating to be connected, to find itself.

House of Bourbon

My mother said
she always felt rich
coming home
from the liquor store.
She got cigarettes there too.
Her wealth was a secret
that couldn't be hidden
in the dark corner
of the kitchen cabinet
where her attention was,
always, above the phone.
She sat there
on a stool. A quick
swipe of lipstick
and her mouth
was a wound.

A Certain Blindness

A certain blindness enables me to see
The details of the picture right here,
The flat white flowers in the lower left
And how the white lifts up from there
Into a stream that cuts a jagged line
Across the landscape, edged with trees
And their rippling counterpart in water.
A wavering version of their upper selves
That, somehow, tells us by reflection
Things can be transformed. Clouds too
Are floating with the trees and bob
With the blackbirds that gather
In a cluster, dark against the white,
Wings wide and warped upon the water.

Voting at the Church of the Annunciation

The way the clouds
moved across the vast
November blue of the sky
like a colt cooped up
too long made me hurry
my pace up the hill
to the church and at the crest
of the hill the two giant Sycamores
had begun their unleafing,
just barely, so the arch
of their branches became separate
not fused undercover of leaves.
They leaned slightly apart
at the top as if to give room
to each other for reaching.
It was a cheerful long line
at the church.
No matter the wait
it had already taken
each of us a lifetime
to arrive at that place

where we were going

to be heard.

I Really Don't Care, Do U?

The First Lady visited McAllen, Texas.
The photo shows her smiling, shaking hands
at the Detention Center with the
Health and
Human
Services Secretary.
They stand in front of an American flag drawn by a child.
Welcome First Lady! It says with a double etched W
and a fat balloon top of exclamation.
The First Lady's broad, jacketed shoulders
block all the letters except 'ady'.

The travel guide suggests
if you have only one day in McAllen
visit Quinta Mazatlan, a Spanish estate
amid sprawling tropical gardens.
It features over 250 species of birds.
And the family-oriented Bill Schupp Park
on 19 acres that offers picnicking,
a fitness trail, merry-go-round
and play areas. The Detention Center

with foil blankets, concrete floors and the sounds

children can make, is closed to visitors.

*Words on the back of a Zara jacket that Melania Trump wore to the McAllen Texas Detention Center.

Yellow Car with Foil Saucers

At LAX Airport Esther Pearl Watson
has a painting filled with things we threw away
and this morning I consider
how acrylic lasts
as long
as memory

and how what lives there loses weight,
floats in a black sky crowded
with one-eyed static flying saucers
watching a two-door rusting car's
left tire
go flat

spread out against an absent street
filled with aimless cups and straws and cans
that hover in the eye as they sink
with the tire's airless weight
into a traveler's
mind.

Esther Pearl has fun when she paints,

litters her work the careless

way we used to out the window

of the car.

Letter to J. Bailey Bush

There is no wind this afternoon
so the Moonflower's face is wide
and smooth and the tight bud
wrapped behind will follow soon.

How does a flower become a fruit,
you asked. How indeed?
Eighth grade science was something
we sat through. We attended

each other more than your lessons,
our ears fully employed listening
to our own swelling bodies.
Billy Licklider in the front row

after listening to the tale
of the pistil, the stamen, the
ripe ovules, spoke for us all:
That is so sci—en—ti—fic.

We didn't want to know, not that year.
You wrote our names on the blackboard

first day of class, standing at ease
and so thin in the suit you wore everyday.

Twenty-four names in neat little rows
while we shifted and shuffled our feet
Your names are your history. What you learn
here will lighten your load,

dropped the chalk on your desk like a coin.

Night of the Falling Stars

You were fully awake as in a dream where everything's clear and you know
what you have been striving to know all your life. What you have always known.

The sand had to be there, under your body giving it place that gave into you
and held you still while the ocean moved its memorial pace like a breath

grown vast on that night of the falling stars.

A friend had turned sixty and you'd found him a poem to honor the risk
he assumed in his work, frontiers he crossed, the leaders whose words

he weighed in ancient cities without tables and chairs for support.
In the poem the poet is suddenly alone under light, under the gaze of guns

on the road, where his name, the make of the car, his reason for travel
become his fate, called through a bullhorn to a circle of troops

ready to unleash their guns aimed at him. Every breath intentional.
A rifle raised in an arc moves him out of the light, back on the road

as he sheds but remembers the tremor of self, the obedient fear.

He is heading towards the poem where it happens again but this time

he knows how it ends.

By the Feel

My grandmother sat at her night table,
shook her head, let her hair fall,
like a horse let loose I used to think
while I watched her lean to one side
as if trying to hear and then to the other
and with long loving strokes
brush her hair. I asked her once
not to do the braid
loving her looseness so much.

There's a knack to doing things right
You go by the feel, she told me, gesturing
with palm up toward the butter, sweating
in a dish on the table. Her hearty hand gestured
each step of churning: how to strain cream,
scrape sides to prevent waste, pour off
buttermilk, add spring water, turn the paddle.

There was a room in my grandmother's house
with no door, a south facing window-filled
room where, with a nurse's quick hands,
she tended a menagerie of plants

whose rubbery leaves sucked

up the air and crept through my dreams.

They seemed to be begging

for something I had but wouldn't give up.

Forsythia

William Forsyth (1737 – 1804)

You gave me your name
   without the long vowel
and a sigh at the end
   to show we are bound.
So speak, would you please
   to the gardener who holds me.
Tell him make my hole bigger
   twice bigger and wider
than a lazy man would.
   My home's in the earth.
No voyager I
   except underground
where soil is my ocean.
   Put me way in the back
or up high on a hill.
   I shout when I bloom
throw limbs in the air
   like a man in a swarm
yelling out loud.

Staircase

Our dreams author us with their certainty
that the home you find yourself in
has forever been home though you search
for the familiar dining room window
overlooking the driveway where your father
drove home at night and the childhood
staircase with sycamore scratching
the landing's window inviting you
to slip out and down into the backyard
where your mother once knelt with marigolds
and never again gave them thought
and without any furniture
or rugs or mirrors to guide you the dream
knows the riddle of the staircase
you are learning to climb.

Elevator

First story

I am in an elevator cut loose falling faster

as it drops, something in my stomach tells

me this and my feet feel strangely unbound.

I am learning something I forgot when

I first fell into light born into weight.

When the elevator crashes and I leap up

just before, do I know it once again?

Second Story

They've been working for months in our building

installing new elevators, first the one to the right

and now the left. I stand at the gaping door

and watch two men joining pieces of machinery

with such intricate skill that I tell them

it's like watching open heart surgery.

They take the metaphor in stride and nod.

Third Story

I am in an elevator with a sliding, folding gate

from long ago. It holds four people closely

and aches open and shut at every floor.

If five crowd in it shudders at the burden
slows its pace and creaks along.
It lets you know what the effort costs
this daily going up and down through walls.

Three

He knew how to sit immovable, a part of the rock he rested on, until the bird, the reptile, the fish, which had retired from him, should come back, and resume its habits, nay, moved by curiosity, should come back to him and watch him.

—Ralph Waldo Emerson, Eulogy for Henry David Thoreau, 1862

The Pianist and the Poet

Seymour Bernstein barely blinks
when he talks, his eyes as at ease
in the light of the world as his hands,
poised over the keys when he asks
us to mark how the note hovers
in air after it's struck so that even
its final hush finds accord. He touches
his student's arm with a gentle continuum,
in perfect concordance, urges her heart
closer to Bach, reminds her to listen,
to breathe, like my poet friend Amy
says in a poem: *Listen. The high kiss
of finch grabs a thread of air.*
This is a transport, rapid as half of a breath
as if ears were satellite dishes on stems.
She teaches too and waits as long as it takes
for her students to hear. She knows
what that means, how it helps to blend
the word and the sound of the word
so the ear and the brain work together.

These tiniest bones hear us think.

Yes, listen to the hush that carries the sound.

*Based on Ethan Hawke's documentary "Seymour—An Introduction"
and Amy Young's poem "Ossicles".

White Morning Light

White morning light rises behind mountains like milk
filling a glass that never spills. Trees stand in shade waiting, silent
as trees, in the absence of light, to show who they are.

Wind through the window keeps its sound secret.
Like hands it turns the leaves up
then over, a quick change of mind.

Half deaf my body strains like a dog on a leash
toward sound which moves through trees
through leaves, long grasses their tassels afloat.

A breeze gives no thought to the whirlblast
of dust in its wake, to the crack of a spark breathed into loud
life, the thick history of a deep-rooted oak struck.

All evidence of the world as it lives
in its backyard so full of fragrance it throbs
as if trying to speak. Are there still people

who knew us as we once were.? Even at night
my good ear hears light. My deaf ear still waits
for the window to open.

People Our Age

I'm a one and only,
I better believe.
Who am I now in this dark hush
of a story?
The mother gone too soon,
the child left alone.
My doctor listens.
The waves from the squeeze
and release of my full-bodied
heart enter his ear.
He closes his eyes
the better to hear.

Santa Barbara Morning

For My Daughters

All crowded today
like an overgrown meadow
alive with color,

with swaying, with sand.
It makes a case for the heart
to open its fist and receive

like they do, the dolphins,
now lifting, wheels turning
their rhythm of breath.

They send and receive
in equal measure.
Sound is their light

that beams through the water,
meets matter that's dense,
copies it home to the brain—

revising, moment

by moment, their place

in this soft constellation.

On First Reading Li-Young Lee's *Eating Together*

I hold the page that holds the poem under my breast
where it rests against ribs. My heart with its resonant
thump makes itself felt in its cage.

Its pulse on the page shakes the words *ginger sesame*
fingers and I feel the warm fragrance of this meal
that a family takes together weeks

after their father dies. Alive, he held his food deftly
between fingers the way my father did.
I know the light touch.

The father dies in the poem *lonely for no one.*

But my father, on a fine June day, went to his office
and shattered his life all over the x-ray room.
Understand how a quiet death blanketed in snow

is music that eases this dangerous lesson.
The notes come from a place where it's possible
to trust the silence that follows.

The Pot that is Boiling

The pot that is boiling is doing

what it is meant to do.

Holding ginger and water together.

This is how we bear losses.

Ginger gives up its heart to heat.

What is released

has been there forever.

Non-Catholic Girl

Misery shaped my body into a ball on the bed
Folding to make my upheaved belly disappear
And quiet its eruption into my throat.

Jesus held up his hand at the end of the hall
Of my school that year and nobody noticed
His barbed wire crown or his cracked heart

As bright a red exactly as the four drops of blood
Like jewels on his robe. He didn't seem to know
What was happening to him but instead

Was waving hello when we marched into lunch.
I thought if I were a Catholic I wouldn't have noticed
Either and wanted to go home.

When I was sick to my stomach I thought of Jesus
How his feet were bare standing on a stone
And I wondered if he had anything inside.

Of him that stung, did his eyes water, did he vomit

Ever? Mine stopped by morning and I scooted

Down the stairs, leaned my head through the railing.

When My Daughter Looks

Cutting a rose in my garden so early one morning
that only the birds and I stirred
in our utterly private world
an eruption of tiny and grave proportions
occurred in front of my face.
A faint movement of air, a wild whirring of wings

and the Hummer and I faced each other.
I held every ounce of my breath,
stood as nearly like stone as I could
while Hummer stayed his ground
took his fill of what he needed
and dashed on to the wisteria.

In a photo of my daughter
she looks into the camera with eyes
that say I am watching but what's more I am seeing.
The shock of that moment is the knowing
that what has happened is all that we want.
All that we need.

Chemo Waiting Room

The chairs are the color of grass.
They line the walls and promenade
down the middle in two rows
back to back. People wait here

but not for long. Why does it
not seem crowded? Sharp-angled
frames of hard wood separate one
chair from the next. Pocketbooks

and cups go on the floor but
not for long. Something new
is to be heard in everyday talk:
I never gave Jim the keys.

And some time make the time to drive out west

Seamus Heaney's *Postscript*

My travel guide, I'm listening, ears abuzz with pleasure
to the easy way you start this poem, which takes me
far from my Ohio phrases, to early fall in Ireland,
dueling light and wind and water, to County Clare
whose name is prelude to a music strummed
on three strings, where water and water
stand side by side, ocean breath by mirror lake
that holds a glare of swans settled in a nest
of wind that stirs them into gleaming froth.
A glanced, momentary world brings forth an urgent rush
from you, this afterthought of ecstasy.

Cautious Trapper

For W.S. Merwin

I love loving him for his breath
Which is there to be found if his words
Are unlocked from the page through my hands
To my heart where a searchlight for pause
Recodes order like a path in the snow
Made by a cautious trapper who knows
Every step of the way through the woods
Even in winter and wind shows its course
Through the dangling dry beech
As a shimmering sound meant only
For this earth this day in these woods

Birds in a Line

Suddenly sand under our feet and ocean
after scarlet fever took us from Ohio
and our dog our swing and our father
who maybe was looking to find us
through wires overhead pinned to dark poles

where birds caught their breath in a line
after flying so far they couldn't see home
not though from lack of light
which crowded the sky
their little feet clutching on tight

so tight they might feel words heading
back along road after road as if they
remembered where they were going
as if where they were going
was still there.

The Hickory Out Front

We come back to how we started to be.
I was a girl with a heart that could break
at the tick of a clock, a knock at the door.

It was time passing that did it.
It hasn't stopped yet. Leaves
change color overnight where I love.

The hickory out front holds onto its green
made greener by the morning-sun glow
of spicebush's numberless tongues.

But hickory holds out against brightness
and cold. Each heavy-hearted leaf
bows into itself until it lets go

into loss and glory. This time of life
never stops changing.
It's in every breath of my breakable heart.

Highway 85 Heading South

It's taking me toward a heartland faster than light
comes and goes between stripes of shadows.
Perpetual trees behind them bear witness
to this passing and passing and passing
at 60, 65, 70 in an effort to outrun inertia
and put something in motion just out of reach.

A quilter stitched a letter from a lover
into one of the stars in her meticulous design
because she couldn't bear the burden of love.
But its longing lasted. When old and addled
she believed the quilt held the heart she had lost
and she ripped open star after carefully stitched star.

We bury ourselves, wouldn't you say
when we tighten the thread against light?
Every breath a tiny choice between pulling
or letting be. The highway heading south
stays open and edged with bright alive woods
that could become gallows or mast.

Three Amazing Things

The sky is a piercing blue but there is no sun.
The light is intense and sharpens the edge of each leaf.

My oldest daughter is busy with clothes.
She is wearing a sweater with a red rose applique
that rests on what looks like a long green tulip leaf.

Tiny stitches hold flower and leaf in place
which expand and contract with each breath that she takes.

She is telling her sisters three amazing things she has done
since she has come for her visit. The first is the sweater.

She sits up on my side of the bed, tells them that somehow
she owns it. I wonder who made it with all of those stitches,

the sweater with the rose which seems to grow larger
in the piercing light. Her sisters understand the other things she says.
I do not. I think they don't notice the stitches that breathe.

There is a ladder leading out of the room which I know is there
if I need it. I stay, as do my daughters, who all look at me

as if they know me.

When the Sun Goes Down

When the sun goes down as it will
a great crowd in the sky spreads
like a solid gone liquid on the edge
of the world.

It is time: this molten light
at the edge, become golden and red,
disappears from our ledge
while we watch, knowing

it will rise like a loaf and knowing
one day we won't. The crowd
is a summons at the end of a party
when you see why you wanted

to be there, and you'd spent
your time lavishly in talk
slightly beside the point.
The splendor is too much to bear.

The Neurosurgeon Teaches

My father taught like someone who remembered
not knowing. This had its comforts.
His effort to be with us in the dark.
He handled brains in his hands.
Mothers held babies like that.
Grey folds and wrinkles, his textbook.
Brains were everyday things to him.
Another kitchen sink, where he stood one day,
telling us how it worked. Showed us with his fist
held high, thumb tucked tight in the fold,
like the limbic system, snug in its place.
Wrist was the brainstem, made our hearts beat,
our breaths breathe. Knuckles the cerebrum,
in charge of our learning, every move that we made.
My brother inched closer, kicked my ankle.
I wailed. Dad walked to the black ashtray
he'd brought from his study. A cigarette
smoked there, all by itself.

Bookmarks

I need two bookmarks for Rumi.
One for my page after page place.
The other to mark what I find
When I open the book like a fruit
I have split and it spills in my hand.
Now I will have forever his sweet
Waterwheel that accepts, turns
Gives away. And all the while, weeps.

Also by Judith Bowles

The Gatherer (2014)

About the Author

Judith Bowles is Ohio-born, Duke-educated, New York-leavened, and Washingtonian by nature. She earned her MFA from American University in short fiction where she has taught creative writing. Two of her stories were selected for the Pen Syndicated Fiction Project. Her poems have been published in *The Innisfree Journal of Poetry, The Delmarva Review* and *Gargoyle*. She says as she's grown older, her work has shortened, "perhaps eventually it will be nothing but punctuation marks."

www.judithbowles.com

Made in the USA
Middletown, DE
28 August 2019